D0730354

The Best Riddles In the World Volume 2

George Tam

Brain Vitamin Publishing

ISBN: 1494734060
ISBN-13: 978-149473406

What kind of coat can be put on only when wet?

Clue 1: It is put on something old.

Clue 2: People often put on more than one coat.

Clue 3: If it is dry, it has done its work.

Clue 4: It can be brushed or sprayed.

Answer: *Paint*

You are in a cold house in the winter. It is dark. You have one match. There is a candle and a wood burning stove. Which do you light first?

Answer: *The match*

If a blue house is made of blue bricks, a yellow house is made of yellow bricks, and a pink house is made of pink bricks, what is a greenhouse made of?

Answer: *Glass*

What has four legs, one head, and a foot?

Clue 1: It has a foot, but it has never owned a pair of shoes in its life.

Clue 2: It has company at night.

Clue 3: It is a cure for those who are weary or exhausted.

Answer: **A bed**

A hole leading in. A hole leading out. We connect to a cavern that is slimy throughout. What am I?

Clue 1: No human or animal can enter it.

Clue 2: It blows hot air like a hot air balloon.

Clue 3: Every man, woman, and child has one.

Answer: **A nostril**

What starts with "e", ends with "e", and contains one letter?

Clue 1: It is white.

Clue 2: It has a flap.

Clue 3: It is made of paper.

Answer: *An envelope*

Two fathers and two sons went on a fishing trip. They each caught a fish and brought it home. However, they brought home only 3 fishes. How could this be?

Answer: *3 people went on a fishing trip, not 4: the grandfather, father, and son. The father is a father and a son at the same time.*

Break it and it is better. Immediately set and harder to break again.

What is it?

Clue 1: Once broken, it's not something you can glue back.

Clue 2: When you break it, others will cheer.

Clue 3: It is full of names.

Answer: **A record**

Round as a dishpan, deep as a tub, and still the oceans couldn't fill it up. What am I?

Clue 1: I have a handle.

Clue 2: I separate things.

Clue 3: I have many tiny holes.

Answer: ***A strainer or sieve***

Two brothers who live on opposite sides of the road, yet never see each other. Who are they?

Clue 1: When one moves, the other moves in the same direction.

Clue 2: They are not mad. They just don't speak to each other.

Clue 3: They are round like a ball.

Answer: *Eyes*

I run over fields and woods all day. Under the bed at night I sit not alone. My tongue hangs out, up and to the rear, awaiting to be filled in the morning. What am I?

Clue 1: I've traveled many miles.

Clue 2: I have only one master.

Clue 3: When I was born, I was placed in a box.

Answer: *A shoe*

You are running a race. You passed the person in second place. What place are you in?

Answer: *Second place, because you were in third place before you passed the person.*

I dig out tiny caves and store gold and silver in them. I also build bridges of silver and make crowns of gold. They are the smallest you could imagine. Sooner or later everybody needs my help, yet many people are afraid to let me help them. Who am I?

Clue 1: I search for holes to fill.

Clue 2: People don't mind that I put them to sleep.

Clue 3: A drill is one of my favorite tools.

Answer: ***A dentist***

A time when they're green, a time when they're brown. But both of these times, cause me to frown. But just in between, for a very short while, they're perfect yellow and cause me to smile.

Clue 1: People say I have a nice curve.

Clue 2: I come in bunches.

Clue 3: Monkeys will go this for this.

Answer: ***Bananas***

What is it that speaks without any words? And can be loudly and distinctly heard? Will drive away friends and foes alike, and is enough to make a stolid man's face alight?

Stolid- unemotional

Alight- light up

Clue 1: It cannot be seen, but you know it is there.

Clue 2: It can be silent, but deadly.

Clue 3: It takes your breath away.

Answer: *A fart*

Who is it that rows quickly with four oars, but hardly comes out from under his own roof?

Clue 1: I was born an egg.

Clue 2: I am cold blooded.

Clue 3: I have no teeth.

Clue 4: Some say I make a good soup.

Answer: *A turtle*

What is it that you must give before you can keep it?

Clue 1: It is only as good as the person who makes it.

Clue 2: Only time can tell what will happen.

Clue 3: It is sometimes given in writing and even blood.

Answer: ***A promise***

Bury deep,
Pile on stones,
My mind will always
Dig up them bones.
What is it?

Clue 1: The older you are, the
more of them you have.

Clue 2: Some good, some bad.

Clue 3: Possible only when looking
back.

Answer: *Memories*

What kind of shower lights up the sky?

Clue 1: It's out of this world.

Clue 2: It has a tail.

Clue 3: A fallen star.

Answer: *Meteor*

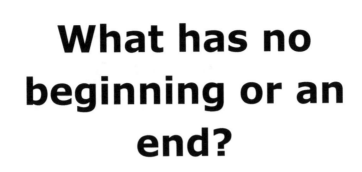

What has no beginning or an end?

Clue 1: * It looks like a letter.

Clue 2: It's a shape.

Answer: ***A circle***

        * the letter 'o'

Take away my first letter, and I still sound the same. Take away my last letter, I still sound the same. Even take away my letter in the middle, I will still sound the same. I am a five letter word. What am I?

Clue 1: bare

Clue 2: deflated

Clue 3: abandoned

Answer: ***Empty***

What is round on both sides and 'hi' in the middle?

Clue 1: A place

Clue 2: United States

Clue 3: Round letters

Answer: *Ohio*

What is it that everybody does at the same time?

Clue 1: Increase

Clue 2: Time

Clue 3: Mature

Answer: ***Grow older***

Paul's height is six feet, he's an assistant at a butcher's shop, and wears size 9 shoes. What does he weigh?

Answer: *Meat*

How many bricks does it take to complete a building made of brick?

Answer: *You only need one more to finish it.*

How many months have 28 days?

Answer: **_While some months have more than 28 days, <u>all</u> of them have 28 days._**

What is red and smells like blue paint?

Answer: ***Red paint***

I make you weak at the worst of time.
I keep you safe, I keep you fine.
I make your hands sweat, and your heart grow cold,
I visit the weak, but seldom the bold.
What am I?

Answer: *Fear*

If an electric train was going east at the speed of 100 miles per hour, which way would the smoke blow?

Answer: *An electric train does not blow smoke.*

What force and strength cannot get through, I with a gentle touch can do, And many in the streets would stand, Were I not as a friend in hand. What am I?

Clue 1: I have teeth, but I don't bite.

Clue 2: I turn left or right.

Clue 3: I can keep you in or keep you out.

Answer: *A key*

You see a boat filled with people. When you looked again, you didn't see a single person on the boat. Why?

Answer: *You realized they are all married.*

A man left home running one night. He turns left and he is still running. He then takes a left again and again. When he arrives back home, he sees two masked men. Who are the masked men?

Answer: *Catcher and umpire. The man was playing baseball.*

What can pass before the sun and casts no shadow?

Clue 1: It is invisible.

Clue 2: It can be felt.

Clue 3: A force of nature.

Answer: *Wind*

A man went for a walk in a forest. When he came back, his car keys were missing. He remembered he had spare keys in his glove compartment. He drove off seconds later. No damage had been done to his car. How did he get in?

Answer: *The car was a convertible and its top was down.*

It can be said:

**To be gold is to be good;
To be stone is to be nothing;
To be glass is to be fragile;
To be cold is to be cruel.
What am I?**

Clue 1: I can become harden.

Clue 2: I can break.

Clue 3: I am a pump.

Clue 4: A symbol of love.

Answer: ***A heart***

What happens when you throw a yellow rock into a purple lake?

Answer: *It splashes, of course.*

Squishes, Squashes, Wishes I washes, Can get it my hair, Makes me not look too fair. What am I?

Clue 1: I am soft and wet.

Clue 2: I am different shades of brown and gray.

Clue 3: I am made of earth.

Clue 4: You sling me when you throw an insult.

Answer: *Mud*

Which side of the turkey has the most feathers?

Answer: *The outside*

You're the bus driver. At the first stop, 4 people got on. At the second stop, 8 people got on. At the third stop, 2 people got off. At the fourth stop, everyone got off. What color are the bus driver's eyes?

Answer: *The same color as yours. You're the bus driver.*

I am the stage
on which dreams are made.
Those who know me would say I am gentle even in a fight.
Though sometimes down, I am rarely out, except when I go camping.
What am I?

Clue 1: I am soft.

Clue 2: I may have feathers, but not a beak.

Clue 3: You rest on me.

Answer: **A Pillow**

What is a question you can never answer "Yes" to?

Answer: *Are you asleep?*

How can you have your feet on both the floor and the ceiling of a large room?

Answer: *You go upstairs directly above where you were downstairs. You will be standing on a floor and a ceiling at the same time.*

There are four brothers in this world that were all born together.
The first runs and never wearies.
The second eats and is never full.
The third drinks and is always thirsty.
The fourth sings a song that is never good.
Who are they?

Answer: *Water, fire, earth, and wind*

A bear that is black is called a black bear, a bear that is brown is called a brown bear. What do you call a bear that is white?

Answer: *A polar bear*

A cloud was my mother, the wind is my father.
My son is the cool stream, and my daughter is the fruit of the land.
A rainbow is my bed, the earth my final resting, place, and I'm the torment of man.
What am I?

Clue 1: I rise and fall, rise and fall.

Clue 2: People run for cover when they see me.

Clue 3: Farmers are glad to see me when I've been away too long.

Answer: *Rain*

A fireman rescues a woman from a burning building and jumps off a 100 foot ladder onto the pavement below. He is completely unharmed. How can this be?

Answer: *He was on the last step of the ladder when he jumped.*

I always go to sleep with my shoes on?

What am I?

Clue 1: I like to race around a track.

Clue 2: I carry a load on me.

Clue 3: I sleep standing up.

Clue 4: I have a tail.

Answer: **A horse**

A horse is tied to a 24 foot rope and wants an apple that is 27 feet away. When the owner of the horse returned, he noticed that it had eaten the apple.

How was the horse able to get to the apple?

Answer: *The rope was tied to the horse, but the rope was not tied to anything.*

A word I know, six letters it contains. Subtract just one, and twelve is what remains.

Clue 1: A group

Clue 2: Donuts

Clue 3: Eggs

Answer: **_Dozens_**

THE BEST RIDDLES IN THE WORLD VOLUME 2

In a one-story pink house, there was a pink cat, a pink fish, a pink computer, a pink chair, a pink table, a pink telephone, a pink shower. Everything was pink.

What color were the stairs?

Answer: *It is a one-story house, so there are no stairs.*

What goes through a door but never goes in and never comes out?

Clue 1: A guardian angel

Clue 2: It fits like a glove

Clue 3: A secret code

Answer: **_A keyhole_**

There is a blue house on the right and a red house on the left.

Where is the White House?

Answer: *Washington D.C. The White House is where the President lives.*

A house with two occupants, sometimes one, rarely three.

Break the walls, eat the boarders, then throw the walls away.

What am I?

Occupant- a person who lives in a house

Boarder- a person who is renting a house

Clue 1: Sometimes I'm spread too thin.

Clue 2: I belong to the bean family.

Clue 3: Jelly is a good friend of mine.

Answer: **Peanuts**

List the following from the lightest to the heaviest: a pound of gold, a pound of feathers, and a pound of aluminum cans.

Answer: *They weigh the same, because a pound of anything weighs exactly one pound.*

Two trains leave the station at the exact same time. They traveled at the same speed, side by side, in the same direction, on identical tracks. However, one train arrived at the station in 1 hour and 30 minutes, but the other train arrived in only 90 minutes. How was this possible?

Answer: *Actually, the two trains arrived at the same time, because 1 hour 30 minutes is equal to 90 minutes.*

What can be measured but has no length, width, or thickness?

Clue 1: It cannot be weighed.

Clue 2: It is ever changing.

Clue 3: It can become negative.

Clue 4: Just ask the weatherman.

Answer: *Temperature*

An airplane was headed to California when it ran out of fuel and crashed on the border between the United States and Mexico. Where would they bury the survivors?

Answer: *We don't bury survivors.*

When I'm metal or wood,
I help you get home.
When I'm flesh and blood,
In darkness I roam

Clue 1: It's a creature.

Clue 2: It's also a thing.

Clue 3: It's used in a game.

Answer: **A bat**

**Tool of thief,
toy of queen
Always used to be
unseen
Sign of joy, sign of
sorrow
Giving all likeness
borrowed.**

Clue 1: It's used to hide.

Clue 2: It is worn.

Clue 3: It's a disguise.

Answer: *A mask*

You came to a fork in the road with two signs. One path leads to your destination, the other to a steep cliff two miles away.

There are two people there standing next to each sign. One is an angel and he always tells the truth, and the other is the devil and always tells lies. What could you do to make sure you get to your destination?

Answer: *Just read the signs. Don't guess who is telling the truth.*

A boat has a ladder that has six steps. Each step is one foot apart. The last step is one foot from the water. The tide rises 12 inches every 30 minutes. High tide peaks in one hour. When the tide is at its highest, how many steps are under water?

Answer: *The boat rises with the tide, so none of the steps will be under water.*

What is made of wood but has never been cut?

Answer: *A tree*

I have 6 faces, But no mouth or nose. I have 21 eyes But I cannot see. What am I?

Clue 1: I get tossed around.

Clue 2: People take chances with me.

Clue 3: Some leave empty handed.

Answer: *A die*

A man driving on the highway at 65 mph passes several cars going 80 mph. How is this possible?

Answer: *He was passing by cars on the opposite side of the highway, not on the same side.*

I move very slowly at an imperceptible rate, although I take my time, I am never late. I accompany life, and survive past demise, I am viewed with esteem in many women's eyes. What am I?

Imperceptible rate- cannot tell how fast

Demise- death

Esteem- admiration

Clue 1: I grow.

Clue 2: ...but I am not alive

Clue 3: I'm straight or curly.

Answer: ***Hair***

I'm named after nothing, though I'm awfully clamorous.

When I'm not working, your house is less glamorous.

What am I?

Clamorous- noisy

Clue 1: I leave people in the dust.

Clue 2: When people say, "you suck", I take that as a compliment.

Clue 3: I'm the good kind of a pick-up artist.

Answer: ***A vacuum cleaner***

What do you save that you try to kill,

Once you've killed it,

you try to save some more?

Clue 1: The more you have, the more you'll waste.

Clue 2: You are always catching up to it.

Clue 3: When you run out of it, you can't buy more.

Answer: *Time*

A father and his son were riding their bikes together when the son got into an accident. The ambulance took the boy to the nearest hospital. The man's son was in the operating room.

When the doctor saw the boy, the doctor said, "I can't operate on him. He's my son!" How is this possible?

Answer: *The mother was the doctor.*

A rooster is sitting in the middle of a roof and lays an egg. If the wind is blowing from East to West, is the egg more likely to fall down the right or left side of the roof?

Answer: *Neither side. Roosters don't lay eggs, because they are male.*

The sun bakes them,

The hand breaks them,

The foot treads on them,

And the mouth tastes them.

What are they?

Clue 1: When dried, they become a snack.

Clue 2: When crushed, they become a beverage.

Clue 3: Too much beverage, you'll see double.

Answer: *Grapes*

**We are very little creatures,
All of us have different features.
One of us in "glass" is *set*,
One of us you'll find in "jet".
Another you may see in "tin",
And a fourth is "boxed" within.
If the fifth you should "pursue",
It can never fly from you.
What are we?**

Clue 1: We make beautiful sounds.

Clue 2: We are letters.

Clue 3: We are found in every word.

Answer: ***The vowels (a, e, i, o, and u)***

Walk over the living, They don't even mumble. Walk over the dead, They mutter and grumble. What are they?

Clue 1: I make sugar.

Clue 2: They change color.

Clue 3: They shield you from the light.

Answer: *Leaves*

Thousands lay gold within this house, But no man made it. Spears past counting guard this house, But no man wards it. What am I?

Ward- to protect

Clue 1: I am a factory.

Clue 2: I am a comb.

Clue 3: I am a queen's residence.

Answer: ***A beehive***

Inside me the adventurous find
Quests and treasures of every kind.
Trolls, goblins, orcs, and ore,
Await within my closed walls,
For all those that wish to visit me.
Your hands are the key
To secrets untold,
And your mind will unlock the door.

Clue 1: * I have a table.

Clue 2: I am numbered.

Clue 3: I can be soft or hard.

Answer: *A book*

   *   * table of content*

A hundred brothers lie next to each other, Each white and fine— they've only one spine. I am the tongue that lies between the two, Remove me to gather their wisdom to you. What am I?

Clue 1: I am a divider.

Clue 2: I am a finder.

Clue 3: I am a reminder.

Answer: ***A bookmark***

I bubble and laugh,

And spit water in your face.

I'm no lady,

And I don't wear lace.

Clue 1: I go with the flow.

Clue 2: I have a pool.

Clue 3: I have a pump.

Answer: *A Fountain*

This thing is a most amazing thing.
For it can be both as sharp as a knife
Or as flat as floor.
And yet, for all it can be,
It is as natural as a bee.
What is it?

Clue 1: I am a sign of the time.

Clue 2: I am the leader of the band.

Clue 3: I'll take you on a musical roller coaster ride.

Answer: **A music note**

What ship has no captain but two mates?

Answer: *Courtship*

What runs smoother than any rhyme, loves to fall but cannot climb?

Clue 1: It can fall down on rocks without getting hurt.

Clue 2: It can freeze.

Clue 3: It can rise.

Answer: ***Water from a waterfall***

What has wings,
But cannot fly.
Is enclosed,
But can outside also lie.
Can open itself up,
Or close itself away.
Is the place of kings and queens,
And doggerel of every means.
What is it upon which I stand?
Which can lead us to different lands.

Answer: *A stage*

If you enjoyed this book, you will also like:

THE BEST RIDDLES IN THE WORLD
(Volume I)